A Tune a Day

A Beginning

SCALE BOOK

by

C. Paul Herfurth

May be used as a Supplement
to any Violin Method

Includes Studies in
Thirds, Arpeggios and
An Introduction to Double Stops
All in the First Position

BOSTON MUSIC COMPANY

FOREWORD TO TEACHERS AND STUDENTS

It is of the utmost importance that the student violinist acquire a thorough knowledge and understanding of scales, thirds, arpeggios, and simple double stops within the range of his technical ability.

The appalling number of failures among violin students is due in a large measure to the lack of a thorough foundation in the art of good violin playing, i.e. position, bowing, correct left hand finger development, and rhythm, all of which must be acquired in the first position. This is the only road which leads to success. With this fact in mind I have confined this book entirely to this fundamental position.

The early introduction to playing double stops is two-fold, i.e. the left hand position MUST be correct, and the even pressure of the bow upon two strings will help to develop the fingers of the right hand on the bow stick for generally good tone production.

The playing of scales, thirds, arpeggios, and double stops in the various keys, will, in addition to developing the ear, give the student excellent routine so necessary for various bowings in string crossing. Particular care must be exercised in holding the fingers down when crossing from one string to another. Smoothness in scales will be the reward.

Another weakness with many violin students is their lack of rhythmic feeling. The various rhythm patterns in connection with the scales should be diligently studied. Many additional rhythm patterns may be suggested by the teacher.

Let us as teachers try to impart to the pupil a feeling for artistic performance. Too many music students, today play by the "hit and miss" method. It is not how much a student can play but how well can he play what little he plays.

C. P. H.

Part 1
SCALE STUDIES
D Major Scale (ascending)
(Two Sharps - F♯ and C♯)

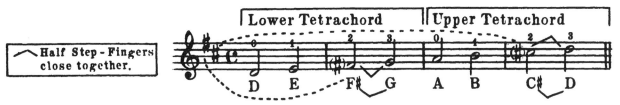

Half Step - Fingers close together.

Learn To Recite All Scales Before Playing.

REMEMBER - What You Can't Think You Can't Play

Think note values and keep time steady.

QUESTIONS 1. Name the Sharps in the Key of D Major _____

2. Write the Key Signature for D Major

3. Half Steps come between _____ and _____

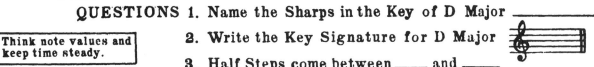

✸ Hold fingers down when crossing to the next higher string.
Rule: Never lift a finger unless you have too.
Learn to play each new scale from memory.

B.M.Co. 11028-25

D Major Scale (descending)

Up and Down the Ladder of D **

Two notes in one bow. Divide bow evenly.

Four notes in one bow.

Three notes in one bow. Notice time signature.

D Major Arpeggio (Broken Chord)

** Piano Acc. Teacher's Manual - Tune A Day - Page 17.
  Melodies in the Key of D Major - Tune A Day - Book I Page 19 - 24
B.M.Co. 11028-25

The Interval of a Third includes three successive letters, if Major, Having the spacing of two Whole Steps; if Minor, having the spacing of a Whole and a Half-Step. Ex. D to F# is a Major Third, two Whole Tones. E to G is a Minor Third, one Whole and one Half Tone.

Broken Chords

Playing on Two Strings (Double Stops)**

** The Bow must remain with equal pressure on both strings, and the tips of the fingers should be placed carefully, in order to avoid touching the next string which is to be sounded.

B.M.Co. 11028-25

A Major Scale **
Three Sharps - F#, C# and G#

QUESTIONS: 1. Name the Sharps in the Key of A Major. _____

2. Write the Key Signature for A Major. _____

3. Half Steps come between ____ and ____
4. Recite the A Major Scale.

Slurred Notes

Two notes in one bow.
Four notes in one bow.

Three notes in one bow. Note time signature.

A Major Arpeggio

** Piano Acc. in Teachers Manual-Tune A Day-Page 30

B.M.Co. 11028-25

THIRDS

Broken Chords

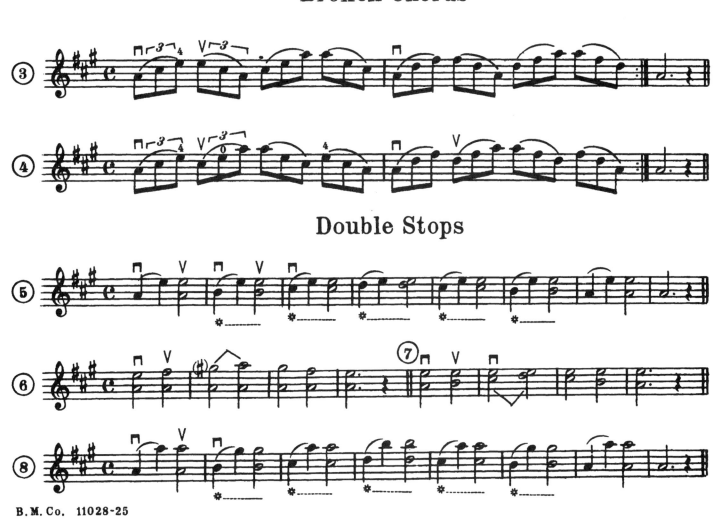

Double Stops

G Major Scale (Lower Octave) ✶✶
One Sharp F♯

Lower Tetrachord | Upper Tetrachord

G A B C D E F♯ G

QUESTIONS: 1. Name the Sharp in the Key of G Major._____

2. Write the K Signature for G Major.

3. Half Steps come between_____and_____

4. Recite the G Major Scale.

Slurred Notes

Two notes in one bow.   Four notes in one bow.

Three notes in one bow.

G Major Arpeggio

✶✶ Piano Acc. Teachers Manuel-Tune A Day-Page 32.
Melodies on Page 26 - 27 Tune A Day- BOOK I.

B.M.Co. 11028-25

THIRDS

7

Broken Chords

Double Stops

PART 2
Second Scale Pattern (Half Steps between the 1st and Fingers)
G Major Scale (Upper Octave)

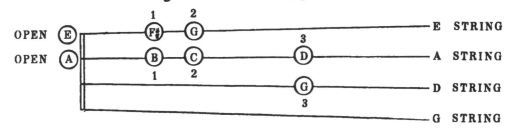

OPEN (E) 1 F# 2 G ——— E STRING
OPEN (A) B C 3 D ——— A STRING
1 2 G 3 ——— D STRING
——— G STRING

Review the questions on Page 6.

Slurred Notes

Combining The First and Second Scale Patterns
G MAJOR SCALE IN TWO OCTAVES

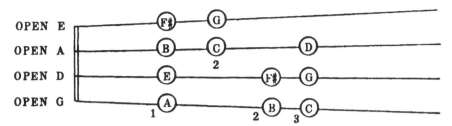

REMEMBER: 2nd and 3rd Fingers close on the G and D String.
1st and 2nd Fingers close on the A and E String.

Broken Chords

THIRDS

B.M.Co.11028-25

SECOND SCALE PATTERN Cont.
Half Steps between 1st and 2nd Fingers
C Major Scale (No Sharps or Flats)✵✵

Slurred Notes

C Major Arpeggio

✵✵ Piano Acc. Teachers Manual - Tune A Day - Page 42
Melodies in Tune A Day Book II Page 8

B. M. Co. 11028-25

THIRDS

Broken Chords

SIXTHS

PART 3
THIRD SCALE PATTERN
Half Steps between the Open String and 1st Finger
F Major Scale (one Flat B♭)**

QUESTIONS: 1. Name the Flat in the Key of F Major._____

2. Write the Key Signature for F Major.

3. Half Steps come between____and_____

4. Recite the F Major Scale.

Slurred Notes

F Major Arpeggio

** Piano Acc. Teachers Manual Tune A Day Page 52
Melodies in Tune A Day-Book II Page 17-18

B. M. Co. 11028-25

THIRDS

Broken Chords

Double Stops

B.M.Co.11028-25

THIRD SCALE PATTERN Cont.
Half Steps between the Open String and 1st Finger
B♭ Major Scale (Two Flats B♭ & E♭)**

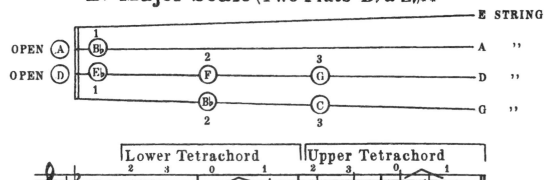

QUESTIONS: 1. Name the Flats in the Key of B♭ Major._____

2. Write the Key Signature for B♭ Major.

3. Half Steps come between____ and____

4. Recite the B♭ Major Scale.

Slurred Notes

B♭ Major Arpeggio

** Piano Acc. Teachers Manual Tune A Day Page 63
Melodies in Tune A Day-Book II Page 24-26

THIRDS

Broken Chords

Double Stops

PART 4
FOURTH SCALE PATTERN IN FLATS
Half Steps between 3rd and 4th Fingers
B♭ Major Scale (Upper Octave)**

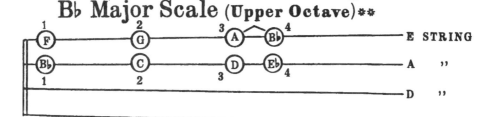

Review questions on Page 14
Cover Two Strings with same Finger.

RHYTHM A

RHYTHM B

Slurred Notes

Two notes in one bow.

Four notes in one bow.

Three notes in one bow.

B♭ Major Arpeggio

Think

Think

B♭ Major Scale - Two Octaves

** Piano Acc. Teacher's Manual Tune A Day Page 63

B.M.Co.11028-25

Broken Chords

In Two Octaves

Double Stops

SIXTHS

FOURTH SCALE PATTERN Cont.
Half Steps between the 3rd and 4th Fingers
E♭ Major Scale (Three Flats B♭-E♭-A♭)**

QUESTIONS: 1. Name the Flats in the Key of E♭ Major. _____

2. Write the Key Signature for E♭ Major.

3. Half Steps come between ____ and _____

4. Recite the E♭ Major Scale.

Slurred Notes

E♭ Major Arpeggio

** Piano Acc. Teacher's Manual-Tune A Day- Page 64
Melodies in Tune A Day - Book II Page 27

B. M. Co. 11028-25

THIRDS

Broken Notes

Double Stops

SIXTHS

B. M. Co. 11028-25

FOURTH SCALE PATTERN IN SHARPS
Half Steps between the 3rd and 4th Fingers
E Major Scale (Four Sharps F♯-C♯-G♯-D♯)**

QUESTIONS:
1. Name the Sharps in the Key of E Major. _____
2. Write the Key Signature for E Major.
3. Half Steps come between ____ and ____
4. Recite the E Major Scale.

Slurred Notes

E Major Arpeggio

** Piano Acc. Teacher's Manual-Tune A Day Page 64
Melodies in Tune A Day-Book II Page 28
B.M.Co. 11028-25

Broken Chords

Double Stops

FOURTH SCALE PATTERN IN SHARPS
Half Steps between the 3rd and 4th Fingers
A Major Scale (Lower Octave) (Three Sharps F♯-C♯-G♯)

QUESTIONS. 1. Name the Sharps in the Key of A Major._____

2. Write the Key Signature for A Major.

3. Half Steps come between_____and_____

4. Recite the A Major Scale.

RHYTHM A

RHYTHM B

Slurred Notes

Two notes in one bow. Four notes in one bow.

Three notes in one bow.

A Major Arpeggio

Broken Chords

Doubles Stops

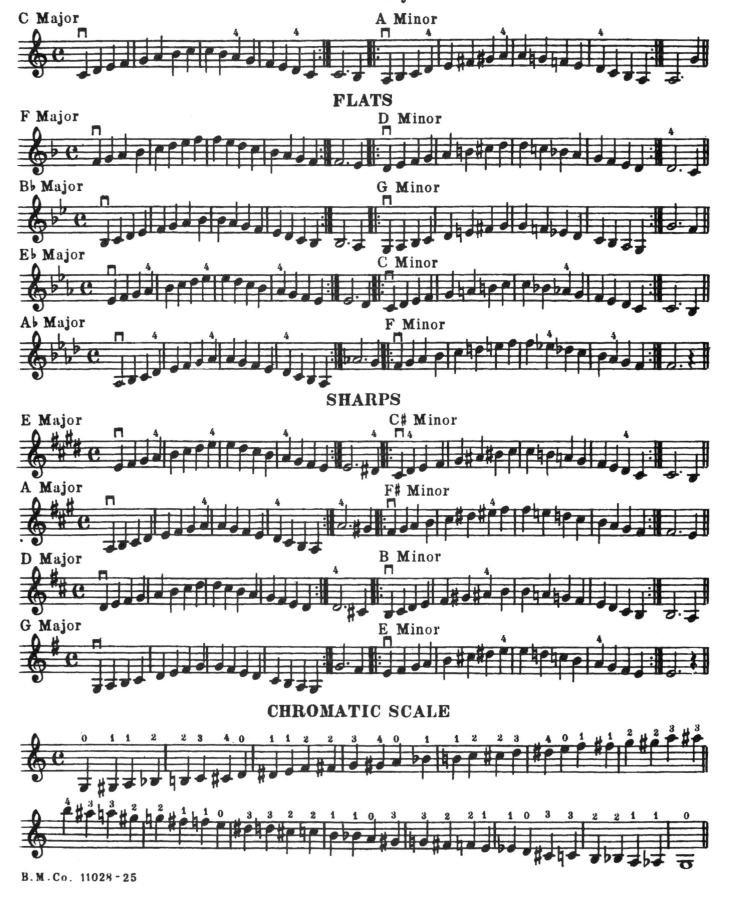

THE MAJOR AND THEIR RELATIVE MINOR SCALES

These Scales are first to be practiced with singled Bows legato, and then are to be played with the following bowings. Slur Two notes in one Bow, Four notes in one Bow, and Eight notes in one Bow. Be sure to divide the Bow evenly.

C Major   A Minor

FLATS

F Major   D Minor

B♭ Major   G Minor

E♭ Major   C Minor

A♭ Major   F Minor

SHARPS

E Major   C♯ Minor

A Major   F♯ Minor

D Major   B Minor

G Major   E Minor

CHROMATIC SCALE

The trill consists of a rapid alternation of the printed note and the next note above, to the value of the printed note. The trill is either a major or minor second above the original note according to the key signature.

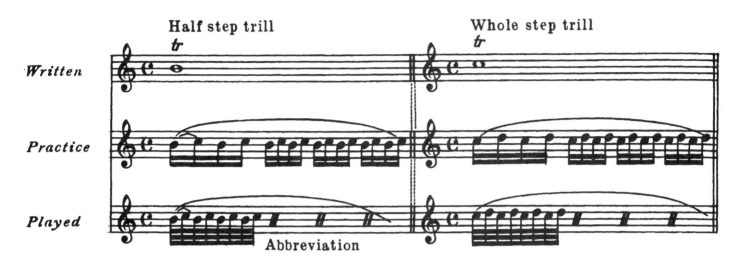

Half step trill   Whole step trill

Written

Practice

Played

Abbreviation

Frequently the trill ends with an after-turn (two auxiliary notes).

Written

Played

Without an after-turn:

Written

Played

If it is necessary to sharp or flat the alternate notes of the trill, a (♯) or (♭) is placed above the trill sign.

Written

Played

B. M. Co. 11028-25